GET READY TO SETTLE BACK ON YOUR
COUCH...BECAUSE MAD IS BLASTING OFF
IN THIS CAPSULE!

In a moment, we're gonna free your mind from
the gravitational pull of such overt forces as
Madison Avenue, Hollywood, TV-land, Publica-
tions-ville and Conformist Suburbia!

STAGE ONE:

We FUEL around with..."*How To Read Graphs*"—
"*Veeble People, A House Organ*" and "*If Comic
Strip Artists Drew Political Cartoons*"

STAGE TWO:

We TAKE OFF on..."*Little League*"—"*Body-
Building and Weight-Lifting*"—"*The American
MAD First Aid Handbook*" and "*Modern Auto
Accidents*"

STAGE THREE:

We adjust our ATTITUDE with..."*MAD'S Cut-Rate
Success Symbols*"—"*Future Halls of Fame*" and
"*The George Washington Advertising Agency Inc.*"

STAGE FOUR:

We make satirical OBSERVATIONS on..."*How
High-Class Magazines Can Use Low-Class
Pictures*"—"*The Battle of the Credit Cards*" and
"*If Famous Authors Wrote The Comics*"

STAGE FIVE:

You experience NAUSEA from... *The Balance of
our Flight into the Ridiculous!*

JUST ONE WORD OF WARNING: YOU'LL
NEED BRAINS — NOT VON BRAUN — TO
TAKE THIS "WAY OUT" LOOK AT OUR
"SQUARE" WORLD FROM...

M A D   I N   O R B I T

AND NOW, IF YOU'RE READY, WE'LL START
THE COUNTDOWN.... Ten...nine...eight
...er...uh...what comes after eight?

More **MAD** Humor from SIGNET

William M. Gaines's

MAD
IN ORBIT

ALBERT B. FELDSTEIN, Editor

A SIGNET BOOK from
NEW AMERICAN LIBRARY
TIMES MIRROR
New York and Scarborough, Ontario
The New English Library Limited, London

SIGNET TRADEMARK REG. U.S. PAT. OFF. AND FOREIGN COUNTRIES
REGISTERED TRADEMARK—MARCA REGISTRADA
HECHO EN CHICAGO, U.S.A.

SIGNET, SIGNET CLASSICS, SIGNETTE, MENTOR AND PLUME BOOKS
are published *in the United States* by
The New American Library, Inc.,
1301 Avenue of the Americas, New York, New York 10019,
in Canada by The New American Library of Canada Limited,
81 Mack Avenue, Scarborough, 704, Ontario,
in the United Kingdom by The New English Library Limited,
Barnard's Inn, Holborn, London, E.C. 1, England

PRINTED IN THE UNITED STATES OF AMERICA

CONTENTS

For a long time, MAD readers have been writing in, telling us of magazines that are much funnier than ours. The only trouble is, they're not sold on the newsstands. They're known as "House Organs," and they're published by and for the employees of giant corporations like United States Steel, International Business Machines, and North American Veeblefetzer. Since you're probably not familiar with United States Steel and International Business Machines, MAD now presents the "House Organ" of the best-known corporation in America:

veeble people

Mr. Elihu Sternwallow, respected President of North American Veeblefetzer, addresses a recent meeting of The 20-Year Club.

Union Representatives leave Mr. Sternwallow's office after having completed successful contract negotiations.

Roto-Polishers Granted Many Benefits in New Contract With North American Veeblefetzer Co.

Mr. Eihu Sternwallow, President of North American Veeblefetzer, has announced the signing of a new Union Contract which, Mr. Sternwallow pointed out, will provide numerous benefits for some three Roto-Polishers employed in the "hashing" room of the Akron Plant in Furdsville. The men are represented by The International Brotherhood of Valve-Lifters, Grease-Sloppers and Loganberry-Pickers, Local No. 528.

Under terms of the new agreement, which Mr. Sternwallow described as the most liberal ever signed in the Veeblefetzer Industry, the men are insured against on-the-job accidents between 2 and 4 A.M. Mr. Sternwallow announced that the Roto-Polishers will not be charged for the extra accounting work involved in deducting the Insurance Premiums from their pay.

The beneficial new contract also provides for the men to receive Half-Pay for Christmas Day, even though they are not required to work when Christmas falls on a Week-End. Also, they will no longer be docked for time lost in going to and from the drinking fountain. Just for the time actually spent drinking.

Mr. Sternwallow also granted the Union a contract-clause which pledges that North American Veeblefetzer will show no favoritism in the matter of Lay-Offs. In the future, all Roto-Polishers will be laid off at the same time.

Other fringe benefits of the new agreement provide for: (1) The company will no longer seek to make a profit in charging the men for the machines they break; (2) Roto-Polishers overcome by Ammonia fumes on the job will no longer be subject to disciplinary action; and (3) Fees for using the company parking lot will only be deducted from the pay of those men who actually drive their cars to work.

Mr. Sternwallow also happily pointed out that the contract calls for an immediate 27¢ hourly wage cut.

In signing the contract, the company agreed to stop pumping tear gas into the 'hashing" room through the air conditioning system. The tear gas was turned on in an effort to help the Roto-Polishers reach a speedy decision on whether or not to accept Management's contract offer.

Mr. Sternwallow Unveils New Models At New York Veeblefetzer Show

Mr. Elihu Sternwallow, beloved President of North American Veeblefetzer, was on hand at New York's Waldorf-Astoria Hotel recently to unveil the firm's 1959 models to Veeblefetzer

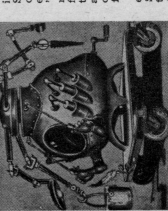

Our New Model 305-J Proved to be the Rage of the Show

buyers from all over the country.

Mr. Sternwallow reported upon his return that our new model 305-J, with self rotating oil cups and horizontal manifolds, was the hit of the show.

In explaining the new North American models to the visiting buyers, Mr. Sternwallow pointed out that the decorative but useless wings placed on earlier models have been removed for '59; that the familiar chrome ornament depicting a Ruffled Grouse in flight has been moved to the rear of the machine for easier accessibility; and that the Air Pressure Gauge is now calibrated in Liters-per-Cubic Meter for greater confusion.

Pop Schlepp Honored After Fifty Years At North American

To the disappointment of some buyers who had been expecting it, Mr. Sternwallow again this year neglected to explain what a Veeblefetzer is used for.

Raunching Rumblings
by Irma Sloven

Seymour Munchner of the Raunching Department became a proud papa for the third time November 8th. This time, the new arrival was a child.

*   *   *

Wilfred Nefty and Helga Prawn of the Raunching Department both took their vacations during the holidays. Quite a coincidence that they both had reservations at the same resort. What about it, kids? Ha-ha!

*   *   *

Reports From The
FRONT OFFICE
by Eloise Schnurd

Mr. Sternwallow is arriving at work these days wearing a lovely pair of orange-and-purple-plaid earmuffs. They make you look years younger, E. S.

Mr. Luther C. Hammerflinger, of Hammerflinger Industries, was a recent luncheon guest of Mr. Sternwallow. Mr. Sternwallow paid the check. Nice going on the generosity, E. S.

Birdie Gruber of the Front Office staff was discharged recently for becoming ill on the job. That's maintaining the old discipline, E. S.

The new "THINK" sign posted by Mr. Sternwallow in the Front Office is drawing a lot of clever comments.

Mr. Elihu Sternwallow, distinguished President of North American Veeblefetzer, was the Master of Ceremonies at festivities on November 5th honoring U. U. "Pop" Schlepp for his 50 years of service with the firm. All employees were docked one hour's pay so they could be present for the gala event.

Mr. Sternwallow presented Pop with a lovely deck of playing cards depicting scenes from Estes Park, Colo., on the backs, and the North American Veeblefetzer Glee Club sang selections from "The Bridge on the River Kwai."

Pop Schlepp joined North American as an Accountant in 1908. He became a salesman in 1922, a Janitor in 1937, and an Assistant Janitor in 1950. In accepting his gift from Mr. Sternwallow, Pop told his cheering fellow-workers that he was looking forward to another 10 years with the company, having given no thought to retirement whatsoever.

He was discharged by Mr. Sternwallow the following morning.

Mrs. Sternwallow Plans Country Club Tea

Mrs. Elihu Sternwallow, lovely wife of North American's youthful President, will be hostess to a Tea and Fan-Tan Game at the exclusive River-Bottom Country Club on December 14th.

No employees of North American have been invited to the event.

Announcement

The Management regretably announces that it is unavoidably forced to call off the First Annual Christmas Party this year.

Reports From The FRONT OFFICE (con'd.)

Mr. Sternwallow's nephew, Irving, who joined the Front Office staff as a junior mimeo operator in October, has been promoted to the job of Sales Manager. It's better than going to college, eh, Irving?

veeble people

Published monthly by and for the employees of the North American Veeblefetzer Co., Squalor Heights, Furdsville, Ohio

EDITORIAL STAFF

Elihu Sternwallow, Jr. ....Editor
Owen "Drudge" Gibbish ....Asst. Editor
Francine La Fleshe ....Sports Editor

Nasty Flipgart vacationed closer to home this year. Nasty reports that he spent a pleasant two weeks renewing old acquaintances at Dirty Otto's Bar and Grill. Nice to have you back with us, Nasty!

*

Wilmer Bzltz will use the money from his Christmas Bonus to buy a new pair of underwear shorts. Wear them in good health, Wilmer!

*

Familiar scenes in the Raunching Department: Emil Snubblefield missing the spittoon . . . Doris Flugert hitting the spittoon . . . Selma Clutz departing early to see her boy friend on "visiting day". . . Slippery Malowick doing his riotous impersonation of Mr. Sternwallow. . . Slippery Malowick receiving his 33rd suspension . . . Imogene Pffeiffeffer getting her hand caught in the stapler . . . Howard Marlin drinking "Moxie."

*

12

Through The Years At North American

5 YEARS AGO THIS MONTH

Mr. Sternwallow increased production quotas in an effort to improve the poor Safety Record rung up at North American Veeblefetzer in 1953 ... The Company's Bowling Team was eliminated when it was discovered that employees could not afford the alley fees ... Mr. Sternwallow announced that Government Regulations concerning the re-hiring of Korean War Veterans did not apply to North American Veeblefetzer ... The First Annual Christmas Party was unavoidably called off.

10 YEARS AGO THIS MONTH

Mr. Sternwallow increased production quotas in an effort to improve the poor Safety Record rung up at North American Veeblefetzer in 1948 ... Employees were ordered to pause for one minute of silence as the last Model 271-B with optional Air Horn attachment rolled off the assembly line ... Employees were docked one minute's pay for non-production ... Mr. Sternwallow announced that he was not interested in Softball, and that the company would not subsidize a team during the coming season ... The First Annual Christmas Party was unavoidably called off.

25 YEARS AGO THIS MONTH

Mr. Sternwallow increased production quotas in an effort to improve the poor Safety Record rung up at North American Veeblefetzer in 1933 ... Pop Schlepp completed 25 years of service with the Company and was presented with a lovely deck of playing cards depicting scenes of Estes Park, Colo., on the backs. At the festivities, The North American Veeblefetzer Glee Club sang selections from "It Happened One Night" ... Mr. Sternwallow announced his refusal to believe that Herbert Hoover had lost the 1932 election ... The First Annual Christmas Party was unavoidably called off.

50 YEARS AGO THIS MONTH

Mr. Sternwallow, a recent graduate of P. S. 47, joined The North American Veeblefetzer Co. as an Efficiency Expert, and immediately recommended an increase in production quotas in an effort to improve the poor Safety Record rung up in 1908 ... Experiments were begun in the Akron laboratory to find a use for the Veeblefetzer ... Management Officials announced that the provisions of the new Sherman Anti-Trust Act did not apply to North American Veeblefetzer ... A suggestion that the Company hold an Annual Christmas Party was adopted unanimously by the employees, and plans were made. However, at the last minute, the Management was unavoidably forced to call it off.

13

The President's Corner

Clumsiness was responsible for this unfortunate accident involving the late Woodruff Durfendorfer, a former employee of North American Veeblefetzer.

Exercise Normal Caution And Help Cut North American's Accident Rate!

by Elihu Sternwallow, President
North American Veeblefetzer Co.

Nearly-complete figures for 1958 tell an appalling story involving the rising accident rate at North American Veeblefetzer. At least 257 employees were injured seriously enough to require hospitalization during the past 12-month period. In many of these accidents, employees had portions of their anatomy caught in the machinery, necessitating costly production slowdowns while they were extricated. In a few cases, the machines were actually damaged and even broken.

Naturally, no firm attempting to return a fair profit to its investors can tolerate the degree of clumsiness displayed by North American employees in the year just ending. Entirely too many of our people are coming to regard their Hospitalization Insurance as an invitation to get injured whenever and wherever they choose. I have already dismissed our Plant Nurse in an effort to put a stop to this attitude, and I will take whatever additional steps may be necessary to bring about an improved record in Plant Safety.

Several employees have come to me recently whimpering that the use of outmoded machinery without safety-guards at North American is responsible in part for the high accident rate. If this were true, and the machinery were to blame, then *all* of our employees would become involved in accidents. Such, of course, is not the case. No less than *five employees*, myself included, went through 1958 without **a** single accident!

We must all work together if North American Veeblefetzer is to improve its Safety Record in 1959. As a first step in this direction, I am increasing production quotas, in the belief that idleness leads to accidents. The rest is up to you. Remember—Safety is everybody's business! *This* business, however, is all mine!

END

WITH A LITTLE BIT OF PUCK DEPT.

Today, the Editorial Cartoonist remains one of America's unsung heroes. (Mainly, we've never heard a single song about an Editorial Cartoonist!) This is because the Editorial Cartoon itself has never quite attained the popularity of, say, the Comic Strip Cartoon. Since Editorial Cartoons are really far more important than Comic Strip Cartoons (and we can't tell you in what way!), MAD feels they could be more appealing . . .

IF COMIC STRIP
ARTISTS DREW

EDITORIAL
CARTOONS

16

"A New Broom Sweeps Clean!"

"Hey, look how this makes him rise again!"

"Ah is caught in a conflik of interests!"

"Leapin' lizards, Daddy,
I wish they'd stop treating me like an orphan!"

"Don't swallow it, sailor! It's no good for you!"

"Atta boy, Joe! Now finish him off with your right!"

Units which have been adopted **Advantages cited**

Since introducti

"C'mon, wake up! Help me get those cookies!"

"Ignore the signs, kid! Keep going!"

END

GRID AND BEAR IT DEPT.

Pick up your favorite newspaper, magazine, or Stockholder Report, and what do you find? Graphs! What are graphs? Graphs are diagrams that show statistics. When are graphs used? Graphs are used: (1) whenever an editor's too stupid to put something in writing; (2) whenever there's an idle artist sitting around; and (3) whenever there's a blank space that needs filling. You can see, therefore, that it is important that you understand graphs . . . especially if you can't read! So, since there's a blank space that needs filling, since there's an idle artist sitting around, and mainly since your editor's too stupid to put something else in writing, here is an article which teaches you . . .

HOW TO READ
graphs

There are several different types of graphs. In order to fully understand each type, first we'll show how each is used, and then we'll interpret the information each type contains. When we're finished, you can explain it to *us!*

THE BAR

THE BAR GRAPH IS HELPFUL WHEN SHOWING

Note how bar graph (below) compares length of Mike's Bar with length of Irving's Bar, bitter next-door competitor.

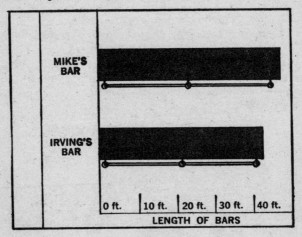

This bar graph compares length of Mike's Bar with length of Irving's Bar after Mike retaliated with some dynamite.

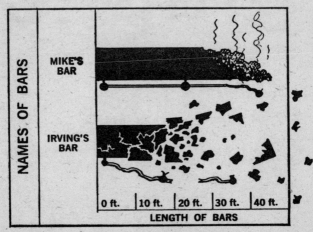

GRAPH

THE COMPARATIVE LENGTH OF BARS

Note how bar graph (below) compares length of Mike's Bar with Irving's Bar . . . after Irving set fire to Mike's Bar.

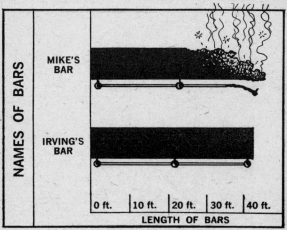

This bar graph compares length of time Mike and Irving will spend behind bars after both were hauled into court.

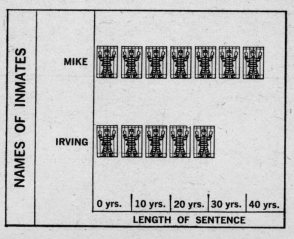

THE LINE

THE OFTEN-USED LINE GRAPH SHOWS

The line graph (below) shows various results attained man tried out his favorite line, "Didn't I meet you

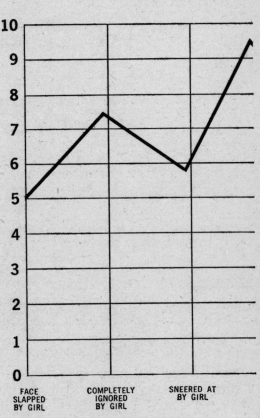

NUMBER OF TIMES THIS LINE USED

| | FACE SLAPPED BY GIRL | COMPLETELY IGNORED BY GIRL | SNEERED AT BY GIRL |

GRAPH

EFFECTIVENESS OF AN OFTEN-USED LINE

with girls on different occasions when Alfred E. New-
somewhere before?"

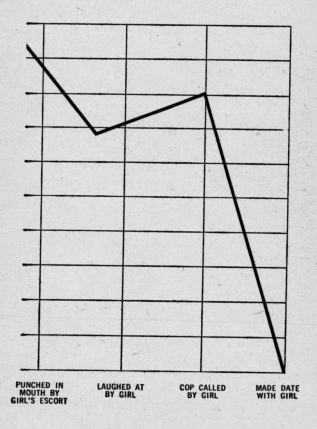

PUNCHED IN
MOUTH BY
GIRL'S ESCORT

LAUGHED AT
BY GIRL

COP CALLED
BY GIRL

MADE DATE
WITH GIRL

THE PIE
THE PIE GRAPH SHOWS HOW ITEMS

Pie graph (below) shows how members of Purple Gougers Gang carved up the pie they swiped from corner bake shop.

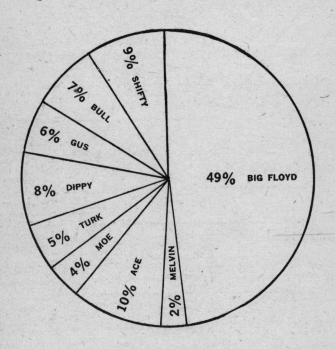

9% SHIFTY
7% BULL
6% GUS
8% DIPPY
5% TURK
4% MOE
10% ACE
2% MELVIN
49% BIG FLOYD

GRAPH

ARE DIVIDED UP, MAINLY ITEMS LIKE PIES

Pie graph (below) shows how rest of Purple Gougers carved
up Big Floyd when he tried-to hog nearly half of the pie.

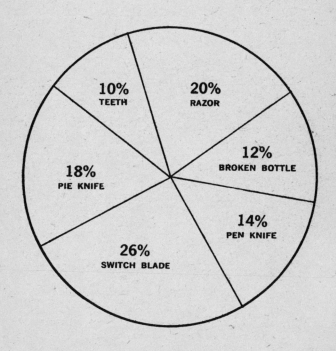

10% TEETH

20% RAZOR

12% BROKEN BOTTLE

18% PIE KNIFE

14% PEN KNIFE

26% SWITCH BLADE

THE PICTURE
THE PICTURE GRAPH IS USED SO CLODS

Note that picture-graph (below) is extremely effective,
long Wembly Beemis stood in Mike's Bar each day from

GRAPH

WHO CAN'T READ WILL GET THE PICTURE

because it gives you a good picture of exactly how
June 2 through June 5.

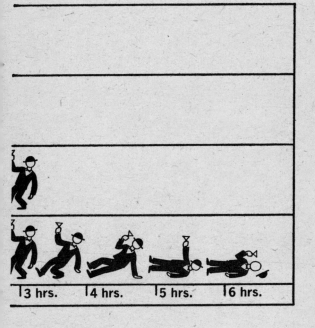

| 3 hrs. | 4 hrs. | 5 hrs. | 6 hrs. |

Note that picture-graph (below) is effective be-
bers of the Purple Gougers Gang who partici-

MONTH		0	5	1
	Jan.			
	Feb.			
	Mar.			
	Apr.			
	May			

Note that picture-graph (above) shows only 6½
ing in rumbles during month of April. Actual
in April after pie caper, proves this is correct.

cause it gives good picture of the average mem-
pated in rumbles from January through May.

0   15   20

members of the Purple Gougers Gang participat-
photo of the Purple Gougers Gang (below), taken
Big Floyd is at right.

END   35

In the old days, whenever a bunch of kids wanted to play baseball, they would gather up some makeshift equipment, hurry on down to the nearest empty sandlot, choose up sides, and have themselves one heckuva good time.

LITTLE

TODAY, MEMBERS OF LOCAL COMMUNITIES THROUGHOUT

Today, this deplorable situation has been eliminated! Because concerned adults have stepped in, organized teams, supplied proper equipment, and now force the kids to play baseball whether they want to or not, in...

LEAGUE

THE NATION ARE GOING CRAZY OVER LITTLE LEAGUE

THE FATHERS

Fathers are going crazy over Little League because they were failures at baseball when they were young, and this is an opportunity to make a comeback through their kids.

The poor Little Leaguer is constantly being pressured by his parents, who expect him to be the 'star'' of the team.

THE MOTHERS

Mothers are going crazy over Little League, hoping maybe one of their men can be a successs, considering their husbands can't make a comeback from where they've never been!

The poor Little Leaguer is constantly being pressured by the sponsor, who expects his team to be League Champions.

THE MERCHANTS

Merchants are going crazy over Little League because, by sponsoring a team, they can plaster their store name on kids' uniforms, making them unpaid walking commercials.

As a result, each week, as the game draws near, the poor Little Leaguer gets keyed up to an anxious fever pitch.

THE POLICEMEN

Policemen are going crazy over Little League because now they don't have to chase the kids from the sandlots. Now they just have to chase them *into* the Little League park.

But, because he's not very good, and the game is close, the coach doesn't let him play. So the *kid* leaves town!

THE FUTURE OF

Little League will get so popular, they'll televise games.

Little League "stars" will be forced to endorse products.

LITTLE LEAGUE

Baseball scouts will search the country for talented kids.

Gamblers will move in, bribing and corrupting the players.

Large corporations, seeking publicity, will sponsor teams.

Sponsors stocks will rise and fall on the outcome of games.

Interest in Big League Baseball will drop off to nothing.

Out-of-work Big League players will lie about their ages.

And when kids want to play baseball, they'll go down to the

League Baseball until the little kids are finally all pushed out.

nearest sandlot and have themselves one heckuva good time.

A NEW
SUPERMARKET
GOING UP
ON THIS
SITE

David
Berg

Some people are world travelers who gather memorable experiences from the far-flung corners of the world. Don Martin's traveling, however, has been limited. And so, therefore, has been his experiences. In fact, he's only had one memorable one in all of his travels:

It Happened On
The
CROSSTOWN BUS

2

3

4

5

6

7

8

9

10

11

12

13

14

15

16

END

NOTHING BUT THE TRUTH DEPT.

The first person we learn about when we study American History is the "Father of Our Country", George Washington. Every school kid in the land knows that George was uncompromising in his truthfulness and honesty. Which brings us to this article. We got to wondering what George Washington would do if, by some stroke of fate, he were alive today. Naturally, he wouldn't stand a chance of becoming President. Who could go that far in politics and still remain honest? As a matter of fact, he'd probably have pretty tough going in whatever he attempted. For example, can you imagine him as the chief executive of a large Madison Avenue corporation called

THE GEORGE WASHINGTON ADVERTISING AGENCY INC.

THE
GEORGE WASHINGTON
ADVERTISING AGENCY

"I cannot tell a lie!"

INTER-OFFICE MEMO

Attention: All Dept. Heads Concerned:
The finalized versions of the following ads are now ready. I have personally checked, edited, and revised them to conform with this agency's policy of honesty and truthfulness. Let me know how the clients react to them.

G. Washington

Chairman and Chief Copy-Writer

ARMSTRONG TIRES'
Ounce of Prevention Grip can save your life

...occasionally!

PATENTED SAFETY DISCS STOP DEADLY SKIDS ... as no other tire can!

(Because no other tire has discs! They may have other devices that work equally well or better, but without discs, they just don't stop deadly skids exactly like our tire does!)

ONLY ARMSTRONG TIRES have unique, patented Safety Discs between tread ribs (arrow).

They keep the tread ribs apart just as discs in the fist keep the fingers apart. Tread can't squeeze shut!

Result: No matter how hard you brake, Armstrong tread stays open, ready to grip the road to stop those deadly skids.

ARMST

Naturally, this lasts only until the tread wears down till it's even with them discs, whereupon it all becomes one smooth slippery surface like any other tire that wears down, with as many skid dangers as ever.

So remember, careful driving is still more important than the tires you use!

LIFETIME ROAD HAZARD GUARANTEE — not 12, 18, 24 months, but as long as you use the tire   . . . subject to very tricky limitations!

Compare the Guarantee Armstrong gives you with that on ordinary tires! (And please note that even though Armstrong is an ordinary tire, we feel otherwise!) "Rhino-Flex" construction makes Armstrong Tires so rugged they are guaranteed for the entire lifetime of the tire (adjust-ment, prorated for used tire tread) . . . and here's the tricky part, because we prorate off the list price and not off the usual discount price, and we have a clever method for measuring tread-use, so you really wind up paying for a new tire even if it blows out while you leave the showroom!

MAKERS OF ARMSTRONG *Pura-Foam* FOR FURNITURE AND BEDDING — HOME OFFICE, WEST HAVEN, CONNECTICUT

59

The fine art of

Staying Lovely

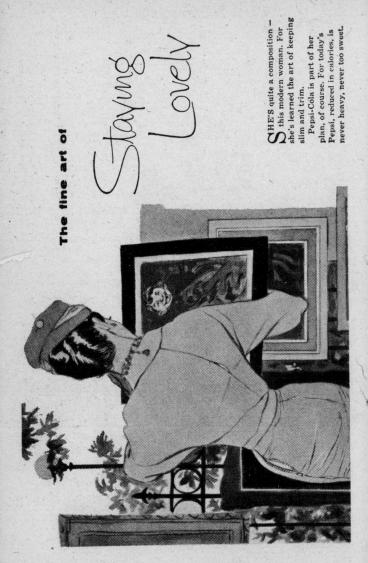

SHE'S quite a composition — this modern woman. For she's learned the art of keeping slim and trim.

Pepsi-Cola is part of her plan, of course. For today's Pepsi, reduced in calories, is never heavy, never too sweet.

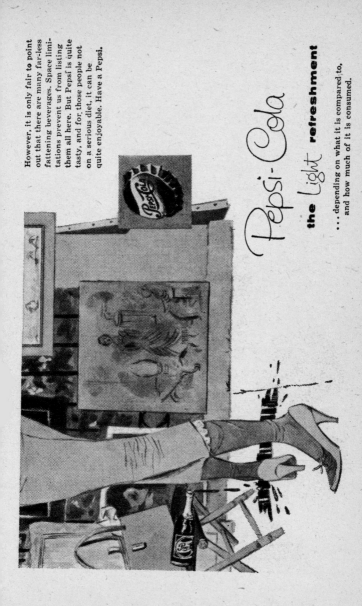

However, it is only fair to point out that there are many far-less fattening beverages. Space limitations prevent us from listing them all here. But Pepsi is quite tasty, and for those people not on a serious diet, it can be quite enjoyable. Have a Pepsi.

Pepsi-Cola

the light refreshment

... depending on what it is compared to, and how much of it is consumed.

62

Light into that Live Modern flavor change to modern L&M

AMANDA BLAKE AND JIM ARNESS TAKE AN L&M BREAK ON GUNSMOKE SET, HOLLYWOOD. THIS IS NOT NECESSARILY INTENDED TO IMPLY THAT THEY ARE SMOKING L&M, NOR THAT THEY EVER DO. THIS MERELY SUGGESTS THEY HAVE TAKEN TIME OUT TO POSE AS PAID MODELS.

*We're still trying to find out who "they" refers to!

63

SUPREMACY

ALMOST...

No other motor car produced today can match the quality and magnificence of the new Cadillac ... with the possible exception of the Rolls-Royce which surpasses it in many respects. However, in a Cadillac, no detail of safety and automotive craftsmanship is overlooked—except, of course, where they add nothing to sales or profits. The owner of a Cadillac enjoys a unique feeling of achievement—which is so essential to all of us these days—particularly those of us with deep-rooted inferiority complexes. For the Cadillac, above all else, has snob appeal. Your Cadillac dealer will be proud to show you this fine motor car—the finest made today—taking into account the inherent limitations of mass-production. In other words you could get a lemon!

CADILLAC MOTOR DIVISION • GENERAL MOTORS CORPORATION

Safety Plate Glass Windows of Cadillacs protect you from rock-throwing peasants.

Cadillac

64

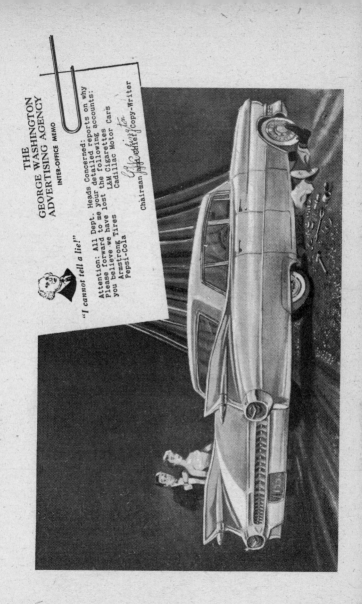

We've decided that the trouble with The Comics today is that they just ain't got no literary value! Things might have been a lot different if they'd started off right in the first place. We're convinced that comics

IF FAMOUS AUTHORS WROTE THE COMICS

would be considered high-class reading matter if only they'd hired some famous authors, poets and playwrights to handle the actual writing. So, if you have a strong stomach, keep reading and see what would've happened

If Paddy Chayefsky Wrote:
DONALD DUCK

If Gilbert & Sullivan Wrote:
DICK TRACY

If Rudyard Kipling Wrote:
PEANUTS

If Walt Whitman Wrote:
THE KATZENJAMMER KIDS

If Rodgers & Hammerstein Wrote:
REX MORGAN, M.D.

THERE'S A BRIGHT GOLDEN CYST
ON HIS ELBOW!
THERE'S A BRIGHT GOLDEN CYST
ON HIS ELBOW!
HIS PULSE IS AS WEAK
AS A DRIED-UP OLD CREEK
AND I THINK THAT HIS KNEECAP
IS STARTIN' TO LEAK!

OH, WHAT A BEAUTIFUL SCALPEL!
OH, WHAT A BEAUTIFUL KNIFE!
I GOT A BEAUTIFUL FEELING
WE CAN STILL SAVE HIS POOR LIFE!

WON'T YOU PASS ME THE NUMBER 5 SUTURE!
WON'T YOU PASS ME THE NUMBER 5 SUTURE!

HIS SKIN'S GETTIN' CLAMMY,
HIS FACE LOOKS ALL WHITE!
AND SOMEHOW I THINK THAT
HE AIN'T BREATHIN' RIGHT!

OH, WHAT A BAD OPERATION!
OH, I WISH IT WEREN'T TRUE!
I DID MY DURNDEST TO SAVE HIM!
LOOKS LIKE HE DIDN'T
PULL THROUGH!

RODGERS
HAMMERSTEIN

If Tennessee Williams Wrote:
LITTLE ORPHAN ANNIE

If Mickey Spillane Wrote:
NANCY

If Edgar Allan Poe Wrote:
DENNIS THE MENACE

Once upon a midnight dreary, while I pondered weak and weary,
Over many a slap and painful spanking that had made me sore —
Suddenly a strange desire prompted me to light a fire,
Flaming higher, fiery pyre — funeral pyre from the floor!
Bright it burned, a brilliant blaze that told me with a final roar
I'd get spankings, Nevermore!

END

One need only to compare the automobiles of
note the amazing progress being made in
compare the files of doctors and hospitals of
pitals today to note the amazing progress

MO

AUTO

yesteryear with the automobiles of today to modern auto designs. And one need only to yesteryear with the files of doctors and hospbeing made in

DERN

ACCIDENTS

THE TAIL-FIN GORE

This mishap usually occurs when unwary pedestrians accidentally back up into parked cars. Also, an increasing number of ruptured stomachs are being reported, too, especially from areas where the lighting facilities are very poor.

THE MANSFIELD FRACTURE

One of the commonest of modern auto accidents being reported, this mishap usually succeeds in shattering the kneecaps, fibula, femur, and shins. Shorter people report having teeth knocked out, and also being stuck in the ear.

THE DOUBLE-HEADLIGHT COMA

Once upon a time, this accident was caused by oncoming "brights." With today's double-headlights, it is now even being caused by oncoming "dims." In fact, a few cases were reported occuring in broad daylight with no lights on.

THE POWER-WINDOW STRANGLE

An increasing number of mishaps caused by this latest innovation in labor-saving devices has been reported, especially among those younger auto passengers who hang out windows. Can be serious if not remedied in reasonable time.

THE HOOD-RELEASE LACERATION

A large number of modern mishaps fall into this category, mainly among service station personnel. Hood acts as if it's stuck, then suddenly springs open, catching victim by surprise—also by chin, nose, teeth, forehead, etc.

THE GAS-COVER AMPUTATION

The high-tension spring which keeps the modern gas tank cover closed contributes much to this injury, but the main damage is caused by the knife-like edges left when the cover itself was stamped out of that metal sheet.

THE LOW-SILHOUETTE CONCUSSION

This accident is usually caused in two ways — entering the car — or leaving it. Bending low is one way to avoid it. However, extreme caution must be used so one does not accidentally strike the face against steering column.

THE POWER-SEAT CONTRACTURE

The majority of mishaps in this category include only passengers in the rear seats being affected. However, some isolated cases are reporting drivers being crushed against the steering wheel and dashboard while moving forward.

THE SWIVEL-SEAT
ABRASION

Not enough reports are available
in this category, as this safety
feature is a relatively new one.
The few that have been received
are almost impossible to believe.
But by using imagination, we can
certainly see the possibilities.

THE SLANT-FENDER
SLASH

Even though this latest design-
style is comparatively new, it
has already chalked up quite a
few surprised victims. It seems
that these razor-edged fenders
neatly slice anyone or anything
that happens to come even close.

GET RICH CHEAP DEPT.

In the old days, our American dream of success was to "keep up with The Joneses." But not any more! Today, our American dream of success is to have "The Joneses" keep up with *us!* Attaining this dream consists of constantly raising our standard of living by attaining material things . . . like new cars, new homes, new furniture, and mainly new ulcers! These things are called "success symbols." Recently, we at MAD figured a way out of this ratrace to attain "success symbols" . . . a way to impress "The Joneses" with things that may *look* expensive, but really aren't! In other words, now we can live beyond our means with no undue strain, thanks to . . .

MAD'S CUT-RATE SUCCESS SYMBOLS

PLASTI-SHAM CADILLAC TAIL FINS
($4.98 per pair)

Full-scale plastic replica — will fool
sharpest eye. Assemble as directed and
place so tail fins extend impressively
several feet past edge of garage door.
End embarrassment of having to drive
beat-up old '49 car. Rich, successful
people always have beat-up second cars!

BOGUS-BOARD ATTIC DORMER
($3.99 each)

Sturdy, weather resistant — will hook easily to any standard house roof, and gives home that "finished attic" look. Invite mother-in-law for lengthy stay to enhance effect. Serves dual purpose by impressing neighbors and irritating mother-in-law who ends up on old couch.

PLEXI-FRAUD AIR CONDITIONER
($2.49 each — De Luxe Model $2.69)

Easily assembled — made of laminated shirt cardboards. Useful for both city and suburban dwellings. Place one unit per window for best impression. Place two units per window for sensational impression! De-luxe model has built-in sponge which drips water realistically.

PSEUDO-FAX HOME IMPROVEMENT SIGNS
($1.95 each — $5.99 the set)

A BRAND NEW
FULLY AUTOMATIC
KASKO KITCHEN
is being installed
HERE
(and it's costing
them plenty!)

A completely new
1962 Model
FALLOUT SHELTER
is being installed in
the basement of
THIS HOME

THIS HOME IS GETTING A
DUCO ENGINEERED
RUMPUS ROOM
Pine Paneling by F. Freem
Inlay Linoleum by Z. Froom
Furnishings by B. Framm
Financing by A. Miracle

Simple, but effective — merely place a
psuedo-fax sign on front lawn for two
weeks, complain bitterly to neighbors
about slow deliveries, work delays,
shoddy materials, etc., then change to
next sign. Made of wood so they can be
burned as fuel after they've been used.

FABRI-TEX SWIMMING POOL
($9.95 incl. installation)

Unit consists of simulated split-wood screen fence with diving-board. Gives impression of big, beautiful backyard swimming pool. Owner can don trunks, climb ladder, and dive off. Owner can also break leg doing this, so safety-mattress is available at small charge.

DECEPTO-PRINT WINDOW SHADES
(89c each — $2.98 the set)

Outside of each shade has full-color reproduction in perfect perspective of room-section with expensive furniture. When entire set is lowered, outsider gets impression of elegantly-furnished home. Also, keeps house dark so you can't see crummy furniture you do own!

UNFORTUNATELY, CUT-RATE SUCCESS SYMBOLS WILL BECOME ACTUAL REAL SUCCESS SYMBOLS

That's right! Word of MAD's clever "Cut-Rate Success Symbols" leaked out, and right now manufacturers are turning out even cleverer ones for those people who will want to outdo their neighbors in faking success.

CORRUGATED FAKE BARBECUE
($2.85 each)

BEAVERBOARD
FAKE BARBECUE
($3.99 each)

DURO-PLASTIC
FAKE BARBECUE
($7.95 each)

GENUINE ALL-BRICK
FAKE BARBECUE
($34.95 each)

SUPER DE LUXE GENUINE QUARRYSTONE FAKE
BARBECUE WITH REAL ELECTRIC ROTATING SPIT
($79.95 each)

END

Today, more and more magazines are discovering that, in order to keep up their high circulation, they've got to print the kind of photographs people want to look at . . . mainly the ones spiced with sex and sensationalism. And this creates quite a problem. Most high-class family-type magazines can't print a picture just for the sake of being sensational! So what can they do? They can phony up a sensational picture with a caption that makes it *look* respectable! To show you what we mean, here are some examples of . . .

HOW
HIGH-CLASS
MAGAZINES
CAN USE
LOW-CLASS
PICTURES

MILLIONAIRE PLAYBOY SHOT BY SWEETIE IN LOVERS' QUARREL

DAILY SPEW Photo by Orlando

Shapely model Zelda Zitzlaff smiles for photogs after pumping five bullets into body of millionaire boyfriend, stockbroker Irving Finster. Shooting took place last night after hour-long argument in Finster's plush East Side penthouse apartment. "The heel didn't come across with the mink he promised, so I plugged him!" confessed Miss Zitzlaff.

Photo as used by HI-FI & MUSIC REVIEW

ORLANDO PIX

Photo as used by BUSINESS WEEK

VICE-PRESIDENCY OPEN AT MYRTLE, LAUNCH

ORLANDO BLACK STAR

Wall Street is speculating as to who will succeed the late Irving Finster (shown above) as Junior Partner, and Vice-President of Myrtle, Launch, Purse, Finster and Beansoup. A veteran of 27 years with the company, Finster served 14 years as Vice-President, after working up from Assistant Ticker-Tape-Tosser. Likely replacement is firm's youngest partner, Campbell Beansoup, son of Melville Myrtle, son-in-law of Otto Launch, and first cousin of Harvey Purse.

Stereo Placement Vital to Proper Sound Convergence

To attain the best results with your stereo system, it is advisable to set up your speaker units so that the sound converges at the point where you will spend the most time. An example of this is shown by the stereo system installed in the penthouse apartment of the late Irving Finster, stockbroker and Hi-Fi enthusiast. Note that the sound converges on the area of the sofa. Equipment includes Dual 24" Hrumph speakers, a Frumpt 7-speed changer, a Mange 5-channel amplifier, a Glick diamond-studded cartridge, and an Atrocious price tag.

Photo as used by SPORTS ILLUSTRATED

JOSEPH ANTHONY ORLANDO

New jewel-handled revolver favored by sportswomen

A new jewel-handled 22 caliber revolver is fast becoming the favorite of sportswomen everywhere. The feminine firearm holds six shells, or five shells and a small lipstick, and measures five inches in length. Small enough to carry in pocket or purse, the weapon is reported to be extremely accurate when fired straight. Other revolvers for women are available, featuring handles inset with pearl, ivory and mink. Created by Miss Ann Wesson, Co.

Penthouse Decorated

The luxury of penthouse living is clearly demonstrated in the apartment of the late New York stockbroker, Irving Finster. Decorated in contrasting tones of lavender and orange, the tastefully appointed living room combines mod-

J. ORLANDO PHOTO SERVICE

ern beauty with Victorian absurdity. Furniture is by Hans
Farshimmelt, carpeting is by Rancid, and draperies are by
The Window. Entire room is set off by Chartreuse-tinted in-
direct lighting. Entire apartment is set off by Dynamite.

JO ORLANDO

SLIT SHEATH
LEADS 1959
FASHIONS

The off-the-back, off-the-shoulder slit
sheath has become a "must" item for
the off-the-nut well-dressed woman.
Exquisitely designed by Pierre Voila in
Paris, this original blend of silk and
burlap is priced at $249.50
(Model: Zelda Zitzlaff)

EARLY VAN DREK PURCHASED
BY STOCKBROKER

ALFRED E ORLANDO

"Barmaid At The Moulin Rouge," painted by the French Impressionist, Scroulous Van Drek, (1850-1950) decorates the New York apartment of the late Irving R. Finster (1900-1959), prominent stockbroker. A well-known collector and art connoisseur. Finster purchased the painting for a price estimated at $175.000, but actually closer to $7.98. The painting is an early example of the artist's work during his Blue Absinthe period.

MELVIN ORLANDO.

The incomparable beauty of the New York skyline at dusk
is captured through the glass terrace doors of a 36th
floor East Side penthouse on a clear Spring morning.

END

CHARLEY HORSE DEPT.

And now, MAD takes a look at the popular pastime which devotes itself to developing and enlarging every bit of body tissue into granite-hard muscle . . . the pastime which frequently goes too far with tissue that never should have been developed and enlarged into granite-hard muscle in the first place . . . mainly the tissue between the ears . . .

BODY-BUILDING AND WEIGHT-LIFTING

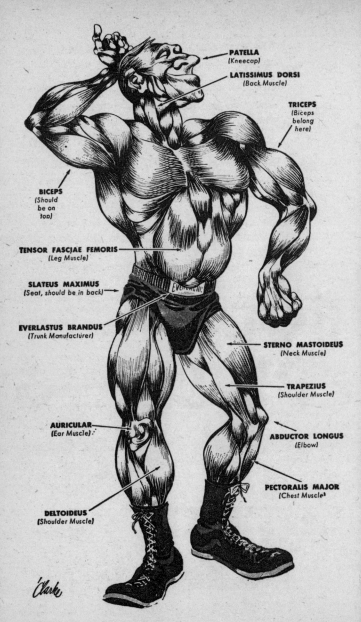

PATELLA
(Kneecap)

LATISSIMUS DORSI
(Back Muscle)

TRICEPS
(Biceps belong here)

BICEPS
(Should be on top)

TENSOR FASCIAE FEMORIS
(Leg Muscle)

SLATEUS MAXIMUS
(Seat, should be in back)

EVERLASTUS BRANDUS
(Trunk Manufacturer)

STERNO MASTOIDEUS
(Neck Muscle)

TRAPEZIUS
(Shoulder Muscle)

AURICULAR
(Ear Muscle)

ABDUCTOR LONGUS
(Elbow)

PECTORALIS MAJOR
(Chest Muscle)

DELTOIDEUS
(Shoulder Muscle)

Clarke

108

The man pictured here is Gus Clutz, undoubtedly the world's most extra-ordinary physical specimen. Through diligent exercising, Gus managed to develop and bring into full bloom every single muscle in his body. Scientists, doctors, and physical-culturists from all over the world have come to admire Gus, to examine and analyze him . . . not because this is the first time anyone has ever developed such perfect muscles, but because Gus has developed all these muscles in the **wrong places!** Please note that this is **not** an anatomical drawing of Gus's muscles underneath his skin. This is a drawing of Gus's muscles on **top** of his skin. Gus is presently on view at Harvard Medical College . . . preserved in a **large jar.**

ADVANTAGES OF A WELL-

The purpose of Body-Building and Weight-Lifting is not to attain a gorgeous physique merely so you can admire it in the mirror while running your hands lovingly over each delightfully pulsating muscle ...

COMMUTING

A good physique looks well when you strap-hang on those crowded subways

BUILT BODY IN DAILY LIFE

nor is it merely so you can go down to the beach and kick sand in that skinny guy's face and embarrass him in front of his girl. Actually, a well-built body is a vital asset in every daily activity.

WORKING

A good physique **performs well** when you have to work in a busy factory.

EATING

A good physique **eats well** when you must dine at a jammed luncheonette.

PLAYING

A good physique **fares well** when you compete in a sport with an audience.

RESTING

A good physique **relaxes as well** as anything so musclebound can relax.

SPECIAL EXERCISES
FOR DEVELOPING
SPECIFIC MUSCLES

Every Body-Building and Weight-Lifting enthusiast knows that there is a special exercise designed to develop each specific muscle in the body. Here is a demonstration of a special exercise designed to develop a specific muscle.

Start to develop shoulder muscles.

Step 1 . . .

Step 2 . . .

Step 3 . . .

Repeat 1000 times and specific muscle (arrow) will be fully developed

114

However, a Body Building and Weight-Lifting enthusiast also knows that extreme caution must be taken to do each special exercise designed to develop a specific muscle exactly as prescribed, or wrong muscle may be developed.

Start to develop knee-cap muscle.

Step 1 . . .

Step 2 . . .

Step 3 . . .

Wrong muscle developed.
Not knee-cap muscle, but
strain-muscle on forehead.

THE HAND GRIPPER
This Spring-Mechanism comes in assorted sizes

"Large" develops both-hand muscles.

"Medium" develops one-hand muscles.

"Small" develops
two-finger muscles.

"Tiny" develops
one-finger muscles.

"Eentsy" develops
fingernail muscles.

COMMON MISTAKES OF BEGINNING WEIGHT-LIFTERS

RIGHT

WRONG

This experienced Body-Building enthusiast performs his weight-lifting exercises correctly...on a concrete floor.

WRONG

This Body-Building beginner makes big mistake, foolishly performs weight-lifting exercises on wooden floor.

TIGHTS

EXTRA

It is important for body-builders and weight-lifters to be fully-equipped for every facet of this invigorating pastime. It is also equally important for body-builders

RUBBING LINIMENT

ELECTRIC HEAT PAD

ASSORTED TRUSSES

PAIR OF CRUTCHES

EQUIPMENT

and weight-lifters to know when to utilize this equipment. Some equipment is for "before"—some equipment is for "after," and below, is some equipment for "too late!"

ELASTIC BANDAGES

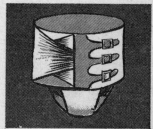

ABDOMINAL SUPPORT

HOME HOSPITAL BED

PAID-UP POLICIES

END

Jack and Jill
Went up the hill
To fetch a pail of water.
Jack fell down
And broke his crown,
And Jill came tumbling after.
     — *Mother Goose*

We've noticed (while looking for ideas to swipe) how every successful magazine has its own distinct style. And it occurred to us how differently each of these magazines might treat the same story. Like, f'rinstance, take the story-poem "Jack and Jill" (and for MAD readers who are unfamiliar with this poem, we have reprinted it at the top): It has a boy and girl. It has romance. It has action, adventure, and even tragedy. It's a natural story for elaboration in different styles. Which brings us to this article, told in MAD's own distinct style (mainly, ridiculous!). So here then, readers, is . . .

JACK and JILL

AS RETOLD BY VARIOUS MAGAZINES

seventeen

"IT WAS MORE THAN A TEENAGE CRUSH..."

Old enough to go drinking in the mountains, but

Too Young To Go Steady

thirty-fourth prize, short story contest

ERNESTINE HEMINGWAY, AGE 17, DWIRP, KANSAS

last prize, art contest

DEENA STONE-MARTIN, AGE 17, MOXIE, VERMONT

Seventeen-year-old Jack had met seventeen-year-old Jill for the first time that summer at seventeen-year-old Camp Sev-Ven-Tee-N, and by the time the seventeenth of August rolled around, they were deliriously in love. Whenever they wanted to see each other, they'd meet behind Bunk 17, because Rule 17 made it a violation for campers of the opposite sex to fraternize. (Incidentally, Rule 18 made it a violation for campers of the *same* sex to fraternize!) But that didn't seem to bother Jack and Jill, because they were seventeen, and deliriously in love. And there were still seventeen days of the camping season left to be together.

They had planned the camping trip to the top of the mountain for weeks, and when the big day arrived, they'd sneaked off separately, and met 17 miles up the trail.

Now, with the bottle of seventeen-year-old scotch Jack had bought with his last $17, they skipped gleefully across the fields toward the mountain, humming selections from the latest Ferlin Husky album. There was a well at the top of the mountain where they could get cool water-chasers.

Little did they realize, as they started up the mountain trail, that the day would end in tragedy for them both, Jack with seventeen stitches in his head, and Jill *(continued on page 17)*

DOUBLE DEATH FOR 2 ILLICIT

Why, when these two young people had almost reached the heights of ecstasy, had brutal tragedy struck?

By Seymour Ghastly, Special Investigator for

OFFICIAL DETECTIVE STORIES

It was Thursday, August 12, 1938, on a hot night just outside Potrzebie, New Mexico. Jack Smith, an itinerant Professional Snooker player, and Jill Jones, his latest girl friend, were making their way slowly up a

Sheriff Roy Sturdley and his deputy were quickly summoned to the scene of the hideous bloody crime.

LOVERS

steep hill to a secluded spot where they could cool off beside a gurgling stream.

Suddenly, about half-way up, Jack felt his right foot slide out from under him. (Subsequent investigation revealed that he'd accidentally dropped his lucky eight-ball, and had tripped over it.) He spun crazily, feeling himself falling. He flailed wildly, reaching out for Jill, trying to stop himself. Instead, he dragged the helpless girl down with him.

Their broken, mangled bodies, battered beyond recognition, and covered with blood (there, we finally got to that word you all love), were found the next morning by 31-year-old Boy Scout, Fred Furd, who was wandering through the woods, trying to find his way back to Denver, Colorado.

At the Coroner's inquest, it was learned that Jack had a Police Record dating back to January, 1932 and had been a *(continued on pg. 59.)*

34567890

Boy Scout Freddy Furd got more excitement than he bargained for on that Saturday hike.

THE MYSTERY PAIL

What secret had the murder victims carried up the hill, then down to their deaths?

TRUE

Lucky for Jack he had a hangnail!

It took raw guts
and nerves of steel
to climb that mountain
— but Jack did it
anyway — thanks to
Jill's raw guts
and nerves of steel!

By
WALTER J. MITTY
TRUE'S
Mountain Climbing
Editor

The mountain meant many things to many men! But to Jack Smith, Soldier of Fortune, Adventurer, and Professional Coward, it meant only one thing. Another challenge! Could he do what no man had ever done before? Could he climb "The Hill?" Would he be crazy enough to try? The answer, as far as Jack was concerned, was "No!"

But the answer, as far as Jill was concerned, was

Aerial photo of mountain peak shows valley spread out below
(Arrow shows bodies spread out below)

THE LAST CLIMB

"Yes!" Jill was Jack's trusted guide. It was Jill who had been responsible for all of Jack's triumphs, all of Jack's successes, all of Jack's fractures and cuts and scars and bleeding. It was Jill who egged him on.

Jack arose early the day of the climb, packed all of his equipment into his lucky pail, and started out. And there was Jill, right behind him, egging him on.

It was fairly easy going at first, but as they neared the top, it soon became slow and agonizing. One false move meant certain death. Many times, Jack wanted to turn back. But Jill kept egging him on heroically.

"I'll wait till she runs out of eggs! Then I'll turn back," thought Jack. But there was no chance of that. Jill always came well-supplied. And so, tortured by wind, pelted by dust, and splattered by eggs, Jack fought on.

Suddenly he screamed.

"Arrr-rrrrr-g-g-g-h-h-h-h

(Continued on page 99)

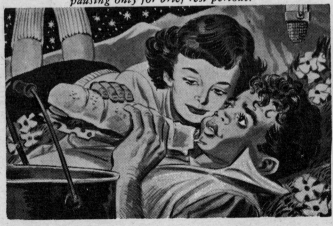

● "I will always love you," sighed Jill, as she wrapped the sardine and cream cheese sandwiches for the picnic outing she'd planned with Jack.

● She watched him as he liberally sprinkled mustard over the sliced tomatoes in the strong masculine way that had won her heart.

"Me too!" he shrugged with virility. He could never find the words to tell her how much he adored her.

The walk up the hill was heavenly. Jill felt warm and secure in Jack's hairy arms. She also felt itchy, but it didn't matter. They talked about the future, about the little 4000-acre farm in Connecticut that Jack would buy when he graduated from Optometry School. They talked about how they'd settle down and raise horses and chickens and cows and Rock Cornish Hens. Nobody mentioned children.

But they were like children, as they skipped along, gig-

They tripped over their feet like two children.

gling and laughing. In fact, they were exactly like children, as they tripped over their clumsy feet.

"Help!", giggled Jill, as she plunged headlong.

"Hoo-Hah!" laughed Jack, as he ripped open his shirt to bare his manly chest, and plunged after her. "I'll save you!"

They tumbled downward together, still giggling and laughing. And as they reached
(continued on back cover)

Confidential

Now it can be told!

Did They Really Go Up For Water?

She bet him he couldn't climb it— and he took her up on it!

The real lowdown on the cutie who made her guy fall ... in a big way!

PROOF!

Hotel Register

Scorecard: four missing teeth, three bruised knees, two lacerated armpits, one empty wallet!

By

ABNER MUCKRAKER

JACK SMITH, THE PLAYBOY with the roving eye who was recently mixed up in a juicy scandal involving a giant, a beanstalk, and a goose (which laid a big egg), will never forget that wild night in Hollywood when he decided to do some "moonlight climbing" with a curvacious little starlet named Jill.

A Wild Night Ahead

The evening began with a stop at one of those famous Hollywood parties, and ended in a knockdown, drag-out, rough-and-tumble slug-fest.

The party had been going on for three days in a Sunset Strip hotel suite, and Jack had taken his blonde cutie there for a warm-up. Then he'd eased her away from the festivities and taken her for a drive . . . up into the Hollywood hills to a secluded spot he knew high above Mulholland Drive.

Using some flimsy excuse about getting water for his overheated Thunderbird, he coaxed Jill up the hill to the spot. All of a sudden *(Continued on page 33)*

The last thing I remember was Jack lunging at me...

I LOVED JACK WITH all my heart and soul and mushy stuff like that, and yet I know now that I should never have gone up that hill with him!

"Don't be a silly fool," he'd smiled. "We're only going up for water!" And he'd taken my hand in his.

I was young, and a silly fool, and I believed him. I'd closed my eyes, fighting reality, fighting my mother's warnings, fighting the cinder in my eye. And I'd gone. I'd gone with Jack. Sweet Jack. Debonair Jack. Jack, with his soft words and his flashing smile, and his snappy blue convertible pail.

It was like a dream. Just the two of us, climbing upward, arm in arm, the wind blowing our hair. I felt as though I was walking on air.

Imagine my surprise when I discovered I really was!

Suddenly, I was falling, and he was coming after me. I felt weak, helpless. Mother had told me there would be moments like this. Unfortunately, she'd neglected to tell me what to do when they occurred. The last thing I remember was Jack lunging at me, and ripping off my *(continued on page 118)*

Jack promised me the stars — and that's what I ended up seeing! But I was too blind with love to listen when

MY MOTHER WARNED ME NOT TO GO UP WITH HIM!

END

It seems like every time we pick up a copy of our favorite newspaper (from the corner trash can) lately, we read that some sport, profession, or group of people has set up a new "Hall of Fame." It isn't enough that they've got Halls of Fame for baseball players, football players, and golfers. Now they've come up with a "Circus Hall of Fame," and even a "Farmers' Hall of Fame." If this keeps up, it won't be long before every glory seeking group in the country will be getting into the act, and then we'll be seeing these . . .

FUTURE OF

AND SOME

HALLS FAME

OF THEIR
MEMBERS

THE LOAFERS' HALL OF FAME

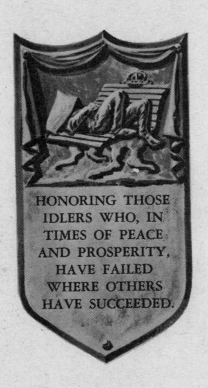

HONORING THOSE
IDLERS WHO, IN
TIMES OF PEACE
AND PROSPERITY,
HAVE FAILED
WHERE OTHERS
HAVE SUCCEEDED.

Member #9—Marvin Mung, of Buffalo, N. Y. During 1945-50 postwar boom, turned down 91 offers of employment, breaking previous record set by Kermit "Drowsy" Fingate in 1920-25. Overslept 457 consecutive days in 1955-56. Is currently thinking about writing autobiography, "Lethargy and Me."

Member #11—Lethargy Mung, Buffalo, N. Y. Only person to be kicked out of a public, private, and military school in same month for class-cutting. Became youngest member elected to Loafer's Hall of Fame in '51, being only 12 at the time. Currently trying to break father's out-of-work record

THE BIRDWATCHERS' HALL OF FAME

HONORING THOSE
HEROIC LOVERS
OF NATURE FOR
WHOM A BIRD IN
THE BUSH IS
WORTH TWO IN
THE HAND.

Member #9—Bessie Clutz, of Oakland, who was honored for heroism on May 6, 1951, when she climbed 12,000-foot Mt. Slagg to observe the mating habits of the Blue-Tongued Eagle. A male eagle spotted her, mistook her for his mate, and carried her off. Neither have been heard from since.

Member #57—Godfrey Lipton, of Wheeling, West Virginia. On July 15, 1954, Lipton camouflaged himself as an oak tree in an effort to better observe a large flock of Pneumatic-Beaked Virginia Woodpeckers. So realistic was his disguise that 5000 of the birds immediately pecked him to death.

THE GARBAGE HALL OF FAME

Honoring those immortals
of Garbage-Collecting
who have distinguished
themselves by their
deeds, and who have
given their profession
a distinctive air.

Member #27—Garbageman Nifty Shlopp, of
Phoenix, Arizona, originator of the famous
Schlopp "Backhand Hoist." This development,
a boon to the profession, now permits our
garbagemen all over the country to dump
their cans with one arm, leaving the other
free to ward off vicious dogs and children.

Member #43—Garbageman Lester "Earplugs"
Rancid, of Tulsa, Oklahoma, who captured
The National Noise Record in 1939 when he
woke up every member of every family in
235 consecutive homes in one morning. It
was Rancid who invented the Galvanized Can
Drop, now used by Garbagemen everywhere.

THE GOSSIP HALL OF FAME

HONORING THOSE
LOOSE-TONGUED
BABBLERS WHO,
BY RUINING THE
LIVES OF OTHERS,
HAVE ENRICHED
THEIR OWN.

Member #7—Mrs. Claudia Culvert, of York, Pennsylvania, whose back-fence gossiping set a new record in 1951 when it resulted in a whispering campaign which broke off 12 engagements, destroyed 17 marriages, and ruined the careers of 39 young men, including that of her eldest son, Irving.

Member #31 — Miss Abigail Sternwallow, of Dwirp, Utah, who was responsible for the tragic Dwirp Disaster. On May 8, 1947, her gabbing tied up all telephone lines, preventing her fellow citizens from being warned of an impending flash flood, which subsequently drowned the whole community.

THE RAILROAD HALL OF FAME

HONORING THOSE
MEN WITHOUT
WHOM THE U: S.
WOULD HAVE
220,000 MILES
OF USELESS
RAILROAD TRACK.

Member #17—Casey Latouche, engineer, who discovered that his Nevada Central freight train, laden with explosives, was 3 hours behind schedule. Disregarding signals, he chose a shortcut down a stretch of single track, figuring to just avoid the oncoming streamliner. He was only four minutes off.

Member #55—Otis Ott, Timetable Editor, who, in May, 1902, made railroad timetable history when he introduced the footnote. Served as roving trouble-shooter, being called in whenever a timetable became too readable. Died at the hands of an enraged mob during 1911 Chicago Commuter's Riot.

THE ADVERTISING HALL OF FAME

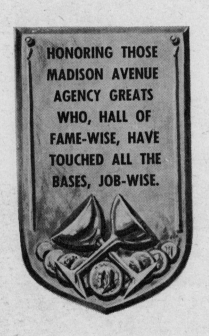

HONORING THOSE
MADISON AVENUE
AGENCY GREATS
WHO, HALL OF
FAME-WISE, HAVE
TOUCHED ALL THE
BASES, JOB-WISE.

Member #5—Felix Hither, of Hither & Yon
Agency. Considered greatest idea man in ad
history. Developed 3-Button Suit in '36,
padded expense account in '40, the triple
martini in '52, multiple ulcers in '54,
bankruptcy of 16 consecutive clients in
'55, and a new form of suicide in 1956.

Member #34—Styles Fernleaf, copywriter
for Stepp & Fetchit. Claiming consumers
should be reached when young, he designed
the first big ad campaign aimed solely at
babies, resulting in such slogans as "The
Gauze That Refreshes!", "Ask The Kid Who
Wets One!" and "Don't Be Half-Chafed!"

THE IDIOTS' HALL OF FAME

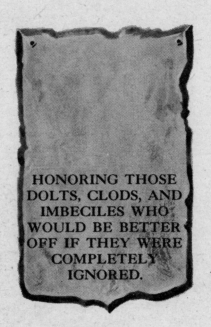

HONORING THOSE
DOLTS, CLODS, AND
IMBECILES WHO
WOULD BE BETTER
OFF IF THEY WERE
COMPLETELY
IGNORED.

Member #6—Melvin Cowznofski. Although barred from 48 states (and Alaska will be voting any moment), he now holds a high position in our country, living atop Mt. Whitney. He currently alternates as business manager of Collier's Magazine, and manufacturing Brooklyn Dodger souvenirs.

Member #1—Alfred E. Neuman, voted "Clod of the Year" four times in succession, has maintained a spectacular record of failure throughout his life. In 1929, he got his first job on Wall Street and immediately caused the crash. Since 1956, he has been technical supervisor at Cape Canaveral, Fla.

Emergencies can occur unexpectedly, at any moment. Are you prepared for them? Do you know what to do when you find someone who has been injured in an auto accident? Do you know what to do when you find someone who has passed out from sunstroke? Do you know what to do when you find someone who has become deathly ill from reading this magazine? If your answer to these questions is "No!", then don't expect any help at all from . . .

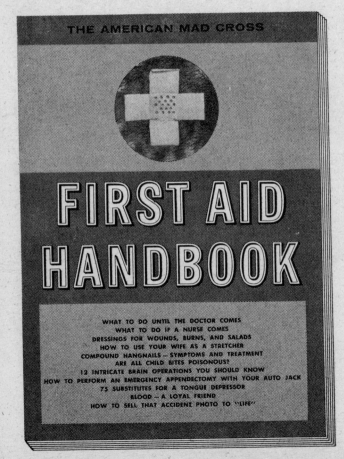

THE AMERICAN MAD CROSS

FIRST AID HANDBOOK

WHAT TO DO UNTIL THE DOCTOR COMES
WHAT TO DO IF A NURSE COMES
DRESSINGS FOR WOUNDS, BURNS, AND SALADS
HOW TO USE YOUR WIFE AS A STRETCHER
COMPOUND HANGNAILS — SYMPTOMS AND TREATMENT
ARE ALL CHILD BITES POISONOUS?
12 INTRICATE BRAIN OPERATIONS YOU SHOULD KNOW
HOW TO PERFORM AN EMERGENCY APPENDECTOMY WITH YOUR AUTO JACK
75 SUBSTITUTES FOR A TONGUE DEPRESSOR
BLOOD — A LOYAL FRIEND
HOW TO SELL THAT ACCIDENT PHOTO TO "LIFE"

TYPES OF BANDAGES

The First Aider uses bandages to hold dressings and splints firmly in place, to provide a clean protective covering for the affected part, and mainly to show the world that the First Aider has been at work. Every part of the body requires its own specific bandage.

The Arm Bandage

The Wrist Bandage

The Finger Bandage

The Leg Bandage

The Head Bandage

The Neck Bandage

THE FIRST AID KIT

Every First Aider should have a First Aid Kit, plainly marked so he can use it to get right up front at the scene of an accident. You can buy such kits from local drugstores, but these are usually badly packed, poorly equipped, and smell like a hospital. The American Mad Cross First Aid Kit, however, is nicely packed, well equipped, and smells like a brewery, mainly because we swiped it from there.

STERILE GAUZE PADS

GERM-LADEN GAUZE PADS

MOUTHWASH

EYEWASH

HOGWASH

SCISSORS

SCALPEL

SAW

HAMMER

UNGUENTINE

OVALTINE

BRILLIANTINE

SINKERS

HOOKS

BANDAGE ROLL

PIANO ROLL

JELLY ROLL

TONGUE DEPRESSOR

TONGUE ELATOR

TONGUE TWISTER

TONGUE SANDWICH

TWEEZER

ASPIRIN

TWEEZER SQUEEZER

TWEEZER SQUEEZER SIEZER

HOW TO STOP SEVERE BLEEDING
Use of the Tourniquet

In cases of severe bleeding, such as after you've tried an improper pressure point, use of a tourniquet may be necessary. The tourniquet should be made and applied with extreme caution, as shown below...

Take length of folded cloth or belt, and wrap around the arm.

Tie ordinary overhand sheetbend half-hitch knot, leaving slack.

Place short stick, preferably teakwood or mahogany, on knot.

Tie bowline stevedore tautline knot around stick and tighten.

Keep turning stick until flow of blood has stopped or . . . ulp!

Quickly untie whole tourniquet! You've put it on the wrong arm!

HOW TO STOP BLEEDING
Use of Pressure Points

In the event that bandages are ineffective, bleeding may be stopped by strong finger pressure on the main artery supplying blood to the wounded part. There are 22 such pressure points on the human body, and it is important for the First Aider to know where they all are.

First Aider places his hand on proper pressure point, stops blood flow from victim's head.

First Aider places his hand on proper pressure point, stops blood flow from victim's arm.

First Aider places his hand on proper pressure point, stops blood flow from victim's leg.

First Aider places his hand on improper pressure point, stops hard slap from victim's hand.

FRACTURES

Fractures can be unpleasant, especially for the person who has one, if you don't know what you're doing. However, they offer the First Aider a chance to shine. Don't be alarmed if you find someone with a fracture. Remember, a bad break for him means a good one for you.

To determine if victim's arm is fractured, first hold arm out in straight position as shown above.

Next, bend arm slowly upward so that it forms a 90 degree angle with original straight position.

If victim does not scream, bend arm slowly back to the original straight position for next step.

Next, start to bend arm downward until it again forms a 90 degree angle with the original position.

If arm does not move easily into final downward position, force it until you hear a sharp crack.

If arm moves easily, it means it was fractured to begin with. In any case, it now needs splinting.

SPLINTS

Once it has been determined that a fracture (or fractures) exists, it is essential for the First Aider to immediately immobilize the limbs surrounding the broken bones. This is accomplished by applying splints to the involved areas. Below are some involved splints.

FINGER SPLINT

ARM SPLINT

LEG SPLINT

THIGH SPLINT

BODY SPLINT

ACCIDENT FIRST AID

Once a First Aider learns, he must practice his training as often as possible. He is sure to get this practice if he is the first person at the scene of an accident. He can be sure of being the first person at the scene of an accident if he is the one that causes it.

ABRASION

Abrasion is always good accident first aid. Try using sandpaper to rub off electrical insulation.

INCISION

Incision is another very common accident first aid. Try cutting the top cellar step with a saw.

LACERATION

A dependable accident first aid, laceration of pipes leading to the gas stove can be effective.

PUNCTURE

Puncture is a proven first aid for accidents. Proper placement of nails and tacks gets results.

FRACTURE

Fracture, an accident first aid that's difficult to trace, can be used on top rungs of ladders.

DISLOCATION

Dislocation is an excellent aid to accidents. Find a sharp turn and dislocate double white line.

WHAT TO DO AT AN ACCIDENT

You discover that a car has gone through a guard rail. You note 2 victims. If you decide that you are capable of rendering first aid, begin treatment immediately.

First make sure victim is alive. Do this by checking his pulse. Remove victim's wristwatch and time his pulsebeat. Then, place his wristwatch in your pocket.

Next, make sure victim is comfortable by removing all objects from his pockets which prevent him from resting easily . . . like wallet, money clip, loose change.

Since man is suffering from minor brain concussion and simple multiple fractures of all limbs, while woman is suffering from a shock, you must treat her first.

Persons suffering shock should be treated gently and kept warm. Immediately find an article of clothing to put around her, and begin treatment to warm her up.

Once she is warmed up, she may need further attention. As this is impossible at the scene of an accident, transport her to place where such care is easily given.

END

Today, more and more business men are using credit cards. A credit card shows that the holder has a charge account like the ones we're familiar with in department stores. Only the whole world is his department store, and things like theater tickets, meals, hotel rooms, gas, etc., are charged merely by flashing his credit card. Afterwards, a single bill is sent out for all these services. However, competition is having a profound effect upon the business. Each credit card company is trying to outdo the other by adding as many services as possible to its system. Here, then, are some of the wonders yet to come to the happy-go-lucky "spend now — pay later" credit card holders, in

THE BATTLE OF THE CREDIT CARDS

OLD FASHIONED successful business man flashes huge roll of bills in a vulgar ostentatious manner to impress people

MODERN-DAY successful business man flashes huge roll of credit-cards in vulgar ostentatious manner to impress people

SOME OF THE RECENT SERVICES LINED UP BY CREDIT CARD COMPANIES SO MEMBERS CAN SAY "CHARGE IT!"

CARDS
EXPENSES
DEDUCTIONS

Let's look at the business expenses during a typical week in the life of a typical business man, and see how credit card statements can be used to prove legitimate expenses.

CREDIT CARD STATEMENT	INCOME TAX DEDUCTIONS	
CHISELERS' CLUB MONTHLY INVOICE	**le J. —OTHER DEDUCTIONS**	
Credit Card #40673	Itemize deductions with explanations of each	Amount of Deduction
Airline Tickets	Business Tra-	
1 Adult $99.50	vel Expenses:	
2 Children $132.75	Airline Tickets	
	for partner	
	and salesmen:	$232.25
Theater Ticket 57.70	Attended Busi	
Cab Fares 4.75	ne s Show to	
Airline Ticket	for parties	
1 Adult 99.50	and salesmen:	232.25
2 Children 132.7		
	Attended Busi-	
	ness Show to	
Theater Ticket $7.70	see Latest	
Cab Fares $4.75	Models:	
	Admission:	$7.70
		$4.75
Hotel Bill no 2		
Honeymoon Suite ... $14.00		
Room Service $62.00	Entertaining	

175

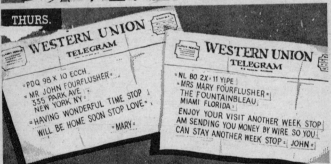

Theater Ticket ... $7.?0
Cab Fare ... $4.75

Admission: $7.?0
Travel: $4.75

Hotel Bill for 2
Honeymoon Suite $44.00
Room Service $103.00

Entertained
Clients:
Hotel Bill: $44.00
Room Service: $103.00

Telegrams
and W.U.
Money Orders $150.00

Business Tele-
grams and W.U.
Money Orders: $150.00

Hotel Bill for 2
Honeymoon Suite $44.00
Room Service $103.00

Clients:
Hotel Bill: $44.00
Room Service: $103.00

Telegrams
and W.U.
Money Orders $150.00

Business Tele-
grams and W.U.
Money Orders: $150.00

Misc. One $2570.00

Gift to Busi-
ness Client for
Closing Big

LEGITIMATE BUSINESS EXPENSES

FRI.

SAT.

TO AIRPORT

TAXI

AIRPORT CAB CO

CREDIT CARD STATEMENT	INCOME TAX DEDUCTIONS	
Telegrams and W.U. Money Orders $150.00	Business Telegrams and W.U. Money Orders:	$150.00
Mink Coat $2500.00	Gift to Business Client for Closing Big Deal:	$2500.00
Car Rental 4 Days $90.00	Business Car Rental:	$90.00
Mink Coat $2500.00	Gift to Business Client for Closing Big Deal:	$2500.00
Car Rental 4 Days $90.00	Business Car Rental:	$90.00
Divorce Litigation Legal Fees ..... $3000.00 Court Costs $700.00	Business Litigation Legal Fees: Court Costs:	$3000.00 $700.00

WHEN THE BUREAU OF INTERNAL REVENUE
CREDIT CARD COMPANIES WILL BE READY

Divorce Litigation
Legal Fees $3000.00
Court Costs $700.00

Business
Litigation:
Legal Fees: $3000.00
Court Costs: $700.00

FINALLY CATCHES UP WITH THIS HORSING AROUND TO OFFER MEMBERS THEIR FINEST ACHIEVEMENT.

END

Recently, we dropped down to our neighborhood fish store, and discovered MAD's maddest artist, DON MARTIN, lounging in the window tank along with the eels. Don was relaxing after a strenuous session pulling wedges out of lobster's claws so they'd be free to tear each other to pieces. While we were waiting for our fillets of guppy, Don told us the following . . .

FISH STORY

1

2

3

4

5

6

7

8

9

10

11

12

13

14

15

16

17

END